IMAGES OF
KENT, SURREY, SUSSEX
& SOUTH LONDON RAILWAYS

IMAGES OF
KENT, SURREY, SUSSEX
& SOUTH LONDON RAILWAYS

HALSGROVE

First published in Great Britain in 2014

British Library Cataloguing-in-Publication Data
A CIP record for this title is available from the British Library

ISBN 978 0 85704 232 3

HALSGROVE
Halsgrove House,
Ryelands Business Park,
Bagley Road, Wellington, Somerset TA21 9PZ
Tel: 01823 653777   Fax: 01823 216796
email: sales@halsgrove.com

Part of the Halsgrove group of companies
Information on all Halsgrove titles is available at: www.halsgrove.com

Printed in China by Everbest Printing Co Ltd

CONTENTS

ACKNOWLEDGEMENTS

I express special thanks to my friends, Mike Daly, Denis Richards and Kenneth Brown for permission to reproduce photos taken by them. Likewise I express thanks for permission to use photos which I have purchased from various collections including the Stephenson Locomotive Society, The Locomotive Club of Great Britain (Ken Nunn collection) and the Stephenson Rail Archive. Also my thanks and apologies are proffered to other photographers whose work has been used and not credited. Where no credit is given the photographer is unknown. I also extend my thanks to Steve Jenkins for advice when describing some of the Carriage and Wagon stock and to Eric Youldon for checking some locomotive details. I am also indebted to Simon Butler of Halsgrove for suggesting the idea of this series of books.

REFERENCE SOURCES

British Railways Locomotive Stock Changes and Withdrawal Dates. 1948 –1968. Michael McManus.

A Detailed History of British Railways Standard Steam Locomotives. RCTS.

GWR, SR, LMSR, LNER and BR Locomotive Allocations for various years. RCTS.

The Locomotives of the South Eastern and Chatham Railway. D. L. Bradley. RCTS.

The Locomotives of the South Eastern Railway. D. L. Bradley. RCTS.

The Locomotives of the London, Chatham and Dover Railway. D. L. Bradley. RCTS.

Locomotives of the L. B. & S. C. R. D. L. Bradley. RCTS.

Locomotives of the L. S. W. R. D. L. Bradley. RCTS.

Locomotives of the Southern Railway. D. L. Bradley. RCTS.

A Locomotive History of Railways on the Isle of Wight. D. L. Bradley. RCTS.

War Department Locomotives. R. Tourret

The Book of the WD 2-8-0s and 2-10-0s. Richard Derry

The Railways Of Great Britain. A Historical Atlas. Colonel M. H. Cobb.

My personal notebooks dating from 1945.

INTRODUCTION

At a very early age I was taken to Dockyard Halt, near Devonport and soon afterwards to St Budeaux GWR station to 'watch trains'. I was taught to remember the names of three engines that passed through. At home there was a Hornby Gauge '0' model railway. Most Saturday afternoons my parents would take me with them from St Budeaux to either Devonport, reached by tram, or Plymouth, to which we caught a 'Motor Train' to Millbay. So my interest in railways steadily developed. During the summers of 1937, 1938 and 1939, the three of us spent a week travelling by train to Torquay, Paignton or Goodrington, with sometimes a venture to Kingswear and across to Dartmouth on the 'MEW' or to Dawlish Warren. We used a Family Holiday Runabout ticket for the week and set out from St Budeaux on an excursion train that ran daily from Saltash to Paignton and which, from memory, was usually hauled by a Castle class locomotive to Newton Abbot. From our front windows at Higher St Budeaux I was able to watch trains in the distance as they climbed towards the Devon side of the Royal Albert Bridge. They could also be seen as they rounded the curves west of Saltash station. I asked my father on one occasion why we did not go to Cornwall instead of to Paignton and he replied that it was better to go up the line. This was probably because there was a daily excursion train from Saltash to Paignton although we sometimes had to change trains at Newton Abbot and cross over the footbridge. My father would bring home books about railways. They had been loaned to him for me to look at and they contained many photographs of railway subjects. During the Second World War, following the second batch of blitz raids on Plymouth when many schools were damaged, I was evacuated to Bude by train from Friary. I stood in the corridor for most of the way to "see where I was going" much to the consternation of the WVS ladies who were accompanying us. I recall seeing a tank engine, at what I later learned was Meldon Quarry, carrying 500S on its tank side. This was the T class 'Service loco'. Whilst at Bude I began to hear about places such as Holsworthy and Okehampton, which I had passed through on the train. Evacuation to Bude was followed by a short period back at St Budeaux after which I spent two years at St Austell, using trains to and from North Road. Whilst there, at the evacuated Grammar school, I met many older boys who were railway enthusiasts and my 'railway education' commenced properly.

My father had been transferred from Devonport to the Dockyard at Gibraltar during 1943, and in the summer of 1947 I went there by sea for a holiday for several weeks. This entailed travelling from Waterloo to Southampton which was my introduction to the SR east of Salisbury.. My father was an amateur photographer and he taught me to use a box camera. I immediately started taking photographs of Gibraltar Dockyard locomotives from a balcony! When I returned my mother met me at Paddington and we stayed overnight with relations who lived near Waterloo. The next morning she gave me a tour visiting London Bridge,

Victoria, Charing Cross, Kings Cross, St Pancras and Euston to introduce me to London's railways. On returning to St Budeaux I found my father's two old cameras and managed to obtain a film for each. A large folding Kodak that used A-122 film turned out to have a pin hole in the bellows, only discovered when the results of the first film were seen. This made it unusable. The other was an old Box Brownie which had a push-over lever shutter release and had one good and one faulty viewfinder that showed two images, one above the other. I persevered with this but did not know enough to achieve much success. I tried to record trains passing through St Budeaux and went to Laira shed late in September and took photos, some against the low evening sun. Still, we all had to learn by experience. With those which I had taken at Gibraltar, this was the start of my collection of railway photographs. I saved my pocket money and managed to go on a few Saturday trips to Exeter and as a holiday treat I was allowed to make trips to Bristol, Salisbury and Cardiff. In December 1947 I did a day trip to Gloucester. In January 1948 my mother and I joined my father in Gibraltar which involved sailing from and to Liverpool. We were routed via the North West route to and from Shrewsbury in each direction. In September 1952 I had my first major 'Railway Holiday' and travelled up the North West route visiting loco sheds en route. My return was by the same route to Newport from where I headed to Lydney on Sunday morning to visit the shed, followed by both of the Gloucester sheds and Cheltenham. In August 1951 I led a small group from Plymouth to London to visit sheds. We had no permits but managed to visit the main SR sheds along with Old Oak, Willesden and Cricklewood. The SR sheds included New Cross Gate which, although having no allocation, hosted several locos in steam and withdrawn locos in store. As we departed from there we encountered the Foreman who ushered us on our way! Later, my employment took me to lodge at St Austell where I finally took up permanent residence. As time progressed I was able to buy better cameras and commenced longer railway trips to places further afield. In the late 1950s I made further visits to SR sheds in London and in September 1958 Mike Daly and myself, each armed with a Seven Day Freedom of the Southern All Line ticket set off from St Budeaux SR to Waterloo where we spent six nights in a hotel opposite the station. We had obtained many shed and Works permits and spent the week covering much of the Central and Eastern Sections of the SR which furthered my knowledge considerably. However Brighton Works eluded us as our week coincided with the annual shut down for the Works holiday. My railway interest widened from purely collecting engine names and numbers to encompass signalling and railway history. This was progressed by meeting more very knowledgeable older railway enthusiasts and railwaymen, many of whom became lifelong friends. I developed a desire to obtain photographs of some of the locomotives that I had seen in my early years, so the process of searching for and purchasing photos commenced. As my interest and knowledge grew, so likewise did the quest for more photos. This now encompassed all of Devon and Cornwall and large sections of Wales, along with various classes of locomotives from all over the country. An interest in Narrow Gauge and Industrial railways developed. So the 'Archive' steadily grew from filling an expanding suitcase to occupying a considerable expanse of shelf space in two rooms. When it was suggested that I compile some books making use of some of these images I thought that it would be a great idea as many of them, to the best of my knowledge, had not previously been used in publications. Previous books covered Devon, Cornwall, Somerset and Dorset, Wiltshire and Hampshire, Lancashire & Cheshire, North and South Wales and the Severn Counties. This is not an attempt to include every location or type of locomotive that has worked in the area but is simply a selection from my collection. As the photos have been collected by me personally my own particular interests and likings for certain locomotive types are reflected by some sections containing larger numbers of photos than others. Some older historic images are included but I have attempted to give a good overall coverage of the area from the 1900s to the present day. A selection of Diesel, Electric and Industrial locomotives is included. I have also used some items which are not photographically perfect but merit inclusion because of their content. A few shots which are slightly outside the named counties are included such as Ascot and Staines which fit in better with this volume than others. South London includes the loco sheds which provided the motive power which worked the lines. These images may be of great interest to modellers of historic locomotives with period layouts. I have attempted to make the captions detailed without delving too deeply into railway history or becoming too technical. As this book features images from my personal collection, the layout follows the order in which the collection is arranged. This follows locomotive wheel arrangement and types from the largest downwards in decreasing order of size, with a few exceptions. It is a system that was used in the past by several notable authors that presents a markedly different layout to the now standard practice of following routes geographically. Readers seeking photos at specific locations should refer to the index of locations at the end of the book. Any errors that are discovered are purely attributable to myself. I trust that within the contents there is material to cater for most railway interests and that memories of a bygone age will be recalled.

Maurice Dart
St Austell 2014

1
LEADERS

One of these controversial 0-6-6-0T locos worked trials in the area from 1949. Two others were wholly and a fourth almost completed. All were cut up during mid-1951.

With its number in a central position on the bodyside 36001 stands alongside Brighton Works in July 1949. Real Photographs Co. Ltd.

Enthusiasts examine 36001 with numbers near each cab as it stands at Lewes in steam on 17 August 1949. E. J. S. Series/R.S. Carpenter Photos

2

4-8-0 TANKS, 2-8-0s AND 0-8-0 TANKS

The 4-8-0Ts mainly worked in Feltham Hump yard but occasionally worked trains to Acton yard. The 0-8-0Ts worked in yards and also worked Transfer Goods trains from Hither Green to Acton yard. LMS 2-8-0s worked in on Goods trains from the ex LMS lines. WD 2-8-0s were on loan to the SR in the mid to late 1940s and worked heavy Goods trains.

Lettered LSWR G16 4-8-0T 493 is at home at Strawberry Hill shed in the early 1920s.

Also lettered LSWR G16 4-8-0T 494 stands in the shed yard at Strawberry Hill in the early 1920s.
Real Photographs Co.

On 1 March 1924 Feltham's rather grimy G16 4-8-0T 495 propels a train over the Hump at Feltham yard past the signal box. H. C. Casserley

Cricklewood's Swindon-built LMS 8F 2-8-0 48414 is on shed at Hither Green on 6 April 1958. It is standing in front of 350hp 0-6-0DE shunter D3098 which was sold to Lanco Railways, Liberia in March 1973. In the left background is C class 0-6-0 31686 which is at home along with D3098. Denis Richards

Ashford's WD 2-8-0 70811 (later 90317) stands in front of an 0-6-0 (possibly a C class) at Hither Green around August 1947. Kenneth Brown

Hither Green's WD 2-8-0 70853 (later 90332) heads a train south between Hither Green and Grove Park between late 1947 and early 1948. S. V. Blencowe collection

A pair of WD 2-8-0s are near the Coal Stage at Hither Green shed on 22 May 1948. The nearest loco, 77259 (later 90216) which was allocated to Bricklayers Arms has been fitted with intermediate positioned lamp irons on the smokebox door for fitting SR headcode discs. W. H. Stone

Two WD 2-8-0s at home on shed at Bicklayers Arms on 22 May 1948 are 77321 (later 90234) and 77311 (later 90226). W. H. Stone

0-8-0T 949 'HECATE' which was obtained by the SR from the Kent & East Sussex Railway is at home on Nine Elms shed in the 1930s where its normal duty was to act as Shed Pilot. It retains the first SR livery with its original boiler which was later replaced with a D1 boiler. I was extremely lucky to see this loco at Easter in 1946 most unusually at Exeter Central. Around noon it was standing in the Up yard partly hidden by the stock of an Exmouth train. I was able to look through the windows of a carriage and clearly read 949 on the tank. It visited Eastleigh Works in March 1946. If locally based Z class 0-8-0T 954 was under repair did 949 deputise for a few days as it was relatively nearby?

Ashford's Z class 0-8-0T 30951 is at its home shed on the coal stage road in March 1951. P. H. Groom

In the mid-1950s Z class 0-8-0T 30952 is at home on shed at Ashford. An N1 class 2-6-0 is to its rear. Rex Conway

Hither Green's Z class 0-8-0T s953 is at home on the coal stage road buffered up to what appears to be an O1 class 0-6-0 early in 1949.

Z class 0-8-0T 955 is at home at Ashford shed in the mid-1930s. On this loco the water delivery feed pipe extends to the top of the boiler.

3

4-6-4 TANKS

These L class locos were mainly used on express services to London from Brighton and Eastbourne. All were rebuilt to Remembrance class 4-6-0s during 1935/36.

Newly built LBSC liveried 327 'CHARLES C. MACRAE' is at Brighton Works yard in 1914. The loco was sent to Brighton shed. Locomotive Publishing Co. Ltd.

Brighton's 328 stands at the outer end of a platform at its home station in the early 1920s. The Locomotive Club Of Great Britain/Ken Nunn Collection.

Brighton's 332 departs from its home station on the 'Southern Belle' Pullman in the early 1920s. Locomotive Publishing Co. Ltd.

Brighton's 333 'REMEMBRANCE' is on shed at Battersea Park in the early 1920s. This shed closed in the mid 1930s. Note the memorial plaque fitted on the tank side below the name. Pamlin Prints

4

4-6-2s

Merchant Navy class Pacifics worked express train to Exeter, Bournemouth, and Dover. Lightweight West Country and Battle of Britain class worked on these routes and also over lines to Brighton and into South and North Devon and Cornwall. LNER locos ventured on to the route to Exeter during the 1948 Locomotive Exchanges. The two Southern Region allocated Britannia class locos mainly worked trains to Dover Marine.

In wartime black livery with its 'Widows Cap' Salisbury's Merchant Navy 21C8 (later 35008 and named 'ORIENT LINE') in as-built condition before naming is approaching Woking on a Down express to the West of England in 1942.

Merchant Navy 21C9 'SHAW SAVILL' (later 35009) from Salisbury shed departs from Woking on an express to the West of England on 16 August 1947. This loco has been preserved. The Locomotive Club Of Great Britain/Ken Nunn Collection

In the mid-1940s Merchant Navy 21C11 (became 35011) 'GENERAL STEAM NAVIGATION' is at home at Nine Elms shed. This loco has been preserved. Colling Turner Photos Limited

In the mid-1940s Merchant Navy 21C13 'BLUE FUNNEL' (later 35013) is near the turntable at Nine Elms shed where it was allocated. Between 20 April and 21 June 1945 this loco carried the name 'BLUE FUNNEL LINE'.
Colling Turner Photos Limited

Recently constructed un-named Merchant Navy 21C17 (later 35017 and named 'BELGIAN MARINE') is at home near the Coaling Plant at Nine Elms shed in 1945. A 21T steel mineral wagon owned by Charringtons is in the right background. Colling Turner Photos Limited

Nine Elms shed's Merchant Navy 35017 'BELGIAN MARINE' (EX 21C17) waits for the road at Clapham Junction on 7 May 1948 as it returned home after taking part in the famous Locomotive Exchanges. It was temporarily attached to a LMS tender to facilitate taking up water from troughs when operating on non-SR routes. E. Foster

Nine Elms shed's rebuilt Merchant Navy 35030 'ELDER DEMPSTER LINES' waits to depart from Woking on 28 June 1958 with a service to the West of England. The front portion of the train is formed from Bulleid set no. 63. A.R. Grierson courtesy of the Stephenson Locomotive Society

Ramsgate shed's newly built un-named West Country 21C129 (became 34029 and was named 'LUNDY') is on shed at Stewarts Lane near the Coaling Plant in Summer 1946. Maurice Dart Collection/Transport Treasury

On 7 August 1949 Battle of Britain 34062 '17 Squadron' (ex 21C162) from Stewarts Lane shed passes Brixton Junction with the Thanet Belle Pullman. This train became The Kentish Belle. Pamlin Prints

Newly built un-named Battle of Britain 21C164 (later 34064 and named 'FIGHTER COMMAND') is at home on shed at Stewarts Lane in July 1946. This was the 1000th loco built at Brighton Works and was the first member of the class to be fitted with the new wedge-shaped cab. When building commenced it was fitted with an original type cab but this was changed to the wedge shape before painting was completed. Real Photographs Co.

Stewart Lane shed's Battle of Britain 34067 'TANGMERE' (formerly 21C167) heads the Kentish Belle Pullman between Bickley and St Mary Cray in July 1955. This loco is preserved and is operational. Brian Morrison/Top Link Photocards

LNER A4 class 22 'MALLARD' (previously 4468), from Kings Cross shed, heads the 12.40pm Exeter Central to Waterloo as it passes through Raynes Park on a preliminary test-run on 8 June 1948 during the Locomotive Exchanges. This famous record breaking loco is preserved and operational. E. Foster

LNER A4 22 'MALLARD' failed following its first runs during the Locomotive Exchanges and was replaced by 60033 'SEAGULL' (ex 4902) from Kings Cross shed. 'SEAGULL' is passing through Queens Road, Battersea with the 10.50am Waterloo to Exeter Central on 10 June 1948. E. Foster

On 14 July 1951 BR Standard Britannia class 70014 'IRON DUKE' is under repair in Brighton Works following problems when wheels shifted on axles. The SR type headcode disc is mounted on a deflector strut and the loco is fitted with the original upright vacuum pipe. The loco is devoid of a shedplate but had been transferred from Norwich to Nine Elms on 10 June 1951. During September 1951 this loco was transferred to Stewarts Lane shed.

In 1952 Stewart Lane shed's Britannia class 70014 'IRON DUKE' is in the yard opposite the coal stage at Dover Marine shed. An arrow is carried below the loco's nameplate indicating that it has worked the Golden Arrow service from Victoria.

Norman Simmons/Hugh Davies Photos

5

4-6-2 TANKS

On the Western section H16 class locos worked as shunters in Feltham yard and also worked Transfer Goods trains from there to Acton yard. On the Central section J class tanks worked trains between Brighton, Eastbourne and London.

Feltham's rather grubby H16 class 516 is in the nearby Hump yard in the early 1920s.

Brighton's J1 class B325 (named 'ABERGAVENNY' until March 1924) heads the Southern Belle past Milepost 19 between Merstham and Redhill in the late 1920s. Pamlin Prints

In the early 1920s Brighton's J2 class 326 'BESSBOROUGH' waits to depart from its home station. The loco lost its name in April 1925. Rail Archive Stephenson (Photomatic.)

6

4-6-0s

These locos primarily worked Passenger trains but mixed traffic classes appeared on Goods and Parcels trains. In their later years even the most prestigious classes could be seen on goods trains.

In the mid-1950s GWR Grange class 6865 'HOPTON GRANGE' is undergoing platform clearance tests in the Windsor line platforms at Clapham Junction. This may have been in connection with forthcoming diversions of trains off the GWR main line between Reading and London and it would be very satisfying to be able to put an exact date on this photo. Another mystery is that the loco is carrying a Southall shedplate and it is not shown as allocated to that depot at any period on Official lists! Lens Of Sutton

In the early 1960s GWR Manor class 7816 'FRILSHAM MANOR' from Reading shed waits to depart from Guildford on an afternoon service from Redhill to Reading. In the right background an N or U class 2-6-0 waits to come 'off shed'.

In the early 1960s Eastleigh's Lord Nelson class 30862 'LORD COLLINGWOOD' works a Down Goods train through Woking. The 2nd to the 7th vehicles in the train appear to be banana vans. For many years this class worked express trains between Waterloo and Bournemouth.

In the 1930s Lord Nelson class A863 'Lord Rodney' from Stewarts Lane shed passes The Lord Warden Hotel and garage as it departs from Dover Marine on a train for Victoria. L. A. Garrard courtesy of the Stephenson Locomotive Society

In the late 1920s Salisbury's King Arthur class E452 'SIR MELIAGRANCE' has been coaled and watered at Nine Elms shed ready for its next duty. Smoke deflectors had not been fitted to the loco which is paired with a Drummond 'watercart' tender.

Without smoke deflectors and retaining a Urie chimney, King Arthur class E736 'EXCALIBUR' is at home on Nine Elms in 1925 fitted with a standard Urie tender. Locomotive & General Railway Photographs/Real Photographs Ltd.

Basingstoke shed's King Arthur class 30747 'ELAINE' is on shed at Nine Elms in the early 1950s fitted with a standard Urie tender. Real Photographs Co. Ltd.

Ramsgate's King Arthur class 763 'SIR BORS DE GANIS' is on shed at Stewarts Lane in the early 1930s fitted with a 6-wheeled 4000 gallon tender. The loco was allocated to Ramsgate shed in 1939. Real Photographs Co.

Un-named King Arthur Class 767 in 'as built' condition was newly delivered to Eastleigh Works in June 1925 from the North British Locomotive Co. The loco was originally to be named 'SIR MORDRED', but as this knight was a traitor the loco was named 'SIR VALENCE'. Fitted with a standard Urie tender, shortly after delivery the loco, which was allocated to Stewarts Lane, is on shed at Dover Marine.

Flanked by a pair of lightweight Pacifics King Arthur class 30795 'SIR DINADAN' from Stewarts Lane shed is on shed at Ramsgate on 1 September 1958. It has been fitted with a standard Urie tender in place of its six-wheeled tender. Maurice Dart

In as-built condition S15 class 510 is on shed at Nine Elms around 1923/24. Locomotive Publishing Co. Ltd./Southern Railway

Fitted with a tender from a Schools class 4-4-0 S15 class 30837 is at home on Feltham shed in 1965. Rex Conway Collection

Hither Green's S15 class 838 heads a mixed Goods along Folkestone Warren in the late 1930s. Tom Corin

Around 1920 T14 class 'Paddlebox' 446 as rebuilt by Urie rests on Nine Elms shed.

Stewart Lane shed's Standard class 5 73042 which was damaged in a crash at Eastbourne is on Brighton shed on 2 September 1958 awaiting moving to Eastleigh Works. To its rear at home is C2X class 0-6-0 32440. Fina Petrol tank wagon No. 220 is on the right. On 25 August 1958 73042 hauling the Glasgow to Eastbourne car/sleeper service ran into the rear of the twelve-car Southern Electric set working the 7.27am Eastbourne to London train in Eastbourne station causing heavy casualties. Maurice Dart/Transport Treasury

Guildford's Standard class 5 73092 is on what appears to be PW train in the siding on the Up side south of Farnham station in 1966. The Electric Car shed is in the background.

7
2-6-4 TANKS, 2-6-2s AND 2-6-2 TANKS

These types were to be found on a variety of services but mainly worked Passenger trains apart from the W class 2-6-4Ts which were used to work Goods services including Transfers to Acton yard. The 2-6-2 included was 'on loan' when the Merchant Navy class were temporarily withdrawn for examination following a derailment.

W class 2-6-4T 1914 is at home on Stewarts Lane shed in the mid-1930s.

Norwood Junction's W class 2-6-4T 1916 is at home around 1946/47.

In 1936 W class Hither Green's 2-6-4T 1925 rests on shed at Norwood Junction. Locomotive & General Railway Photographs/ Real Photographs Co.

K class 2-6-4T 790 (named 'RIVER AVON' in January 1925) is on shed at Tonbridge on 31 May 1919. In June 1928 this loco was rebuilt to U class 2-6-0 790 and was de-named. The Locomotive Club Of Great Britain/Ken Nunn Collection

LMS Fairburn 4MT 2-6-4T 42102 approaches Oxted with empty coaching stock for London formed from Maunsell set No. 942 as E4 class 0-6-2T 32581 enters on a short local train in June 1959. Both locos were allocated to Tunbridge Wells West shed. Derek Cross/Top Link Photocards

In August 1953 Standard class 4 2-6-4T 80033 from Brighton shed has arrived on a train at its home station. Edward Dart

LNER V2 class 2-6-2 60916 (formerly 4887) from New England shed, Peterborough waits at the junction of the lines from Nine Elms shed to run to Waterloo to work the 9am express to Exeter Central in May 1953. This loco worked from Nine Elms shed for a couple of months whilst the Merchant Navy Pacifics were withdrawn for examination following a derailment. Kenneth Brown

Nine Elms shed's Standard class 3 2-6-2T 82021 was withdrawn on 17 October 1965. On 7 November 1965 it is dumped at Feltham shed. Maurice Dart

Ashford's Standard class 2 2-6-2T 84021 awaits departure from Ramsgate station with BR Standard set No. 530 in the late 1950s. David Lawrence/Hugh Davies Photos

8

2-6-0s

These types were all classed as mixed traffic locos and worked a variety of trains.

In the mid-1920s N class A817 is on shed at New Cross Gate.

With a tender blank, apart from a loco number, and carrying a SE&CR plate on the cabside N class 820 is ready to go off Bricklayers Arms shed in the early 1920s as the crew pose for the photographer.

On 1 September 1958 rather scruffy N class 31848 is at home on shed at Ashford. Usually when a loco is not very clean it is a sign that it is a good engine as it spends little time on shed. This was the first member of the class to be rebuilt with a modified Front End. This loco had previously spent several years at Exmouth Junction shed so was familiar to me.

Maurice Dart/Transport Treasury

Guildford's N class 31858 shunts a van train at Farnham on 16 June 1965.

New Cross Gate shed is host to Redhill's N class 31863 in February 1949. Fourteen months after Nationalisation the tender is still inscribed SOUTHERN in SR 'Sunshine' lettering. R. K. Blencowe Collection

On 19 March 1962 Eastleigh's U class 31791 pauses between shunting at Farnham.

U class 31803 presents an atmospheric scene as it oozes steam at home inside the back of Guildford shed mid-afternoon on 7 November 1965.
Denis Richards

A pair of 3-cylinder Moguls stand alongside the turntable at Ashford shed on 1 September 1958. Nearest is N1 class 31877 from Hither Green. In the background is U1 class 31901 from Bricklayers Arms. Maurice Dart

Rather clean U1 class 31899 is at home on shed at Redhill in 1951.

Three locos are at home on Nine Elms on 12 November 1961. To the fore is U1 class 31908. In the left background is rebuilt Merchant Navy 4-6-2 35001 'CHANNEL PACKET' (ex 21C1) while on the right is the front of Schools class 4-4-0 30935 'SEVENOAKS'. Maurice Dart

Two locos are at home on New Cross Gate shed on 20 March 1948. On the left is D1 class 0-4-2T 2253 which was withdrawn in October 1949. K class Mogul 2351 is the main subject of the photograph. R. J. Buckley/Initial Photographics

Brighton's K class Mogul 32338 is at home on 2 September 1958. To its right is U1 class 31902 from Bricklayers Arms. A Southern Electric set is in the background at a platform. Maurice Dart/Transport Treasury

Two locos on shed at Ashford on 1 September 1958 are K class 32339 from Brighton and L class 4-4-0 from Tonbridge shed. In the left background are a Mogul and a C2X class 0-6-0. Maurice Dart/Transport Treasury

Heading the LCGB's South Western Suburban Railtour through Staines on 5 February 1967 is Guildford's Standard class 3 77014.

9

0-6-4 TANKS

These locos worked local and branch Passenger trains.

J class 1597 from Ashford shed brings a local Passenger train into Kemsing on 27 April 1938.

Ashford's J class 31599 is at its home shed alongside the coal stage in April 1949. Withdrawal occurred in November of that year.

10

0-6-2 TANKS

These versatile locos could be found shunting in Goods yards or working local and branch Passenger and Goods trains.

Brighton's E3 class 32165 shunts vans at its home station in August 1953. 6-Pul Southern Electric set 3018 is on the right. Edward Dart/Transport Treasury

At home in the yard at Brighton shed on 2 September 1958 is E3 class 32166. On the right is Standard class 4 2-6-4T 80010 from Tunbridge Wells West. Maurice Dart/ Transport Treasury

Two locos working in Bricklayers Arms Goods yard around 1920 are E4 class 504 'CHILWORTH' and E1 class 138 'MACON' which was withdrawn in February 1933. F. Moore's Railway Photographs/ Locomotive Publishing Co. Ltd.

Three locos are at home at Nine Elms on 12 November 1961. On the left are E4 class 32557 and 32498. On the right is rebuilt Merchant Navy 4-6-2 35001 'CHANNEL PACKET' (ex 21C1). Maurice Dart/Transport Treasury

In the early 1950s Tonbridge's E4 class 32578 stands against buffers at Ashford shed.

Tunbridge Wells West shed's E4 32581 rests between duties at its home station on 3 September 1958. Maurice Dart/Transport Treasury

On 7 March 1938 E4X class 2478 is at home at Norwood Junction shed. In the left background is New Cross Gate shed's E6 class 2414. A. E. Hurst

New Cross Gate shed's E5X class 2576 is on shed at Brighton in the late 1930s.

In 1923 E5X class 586 waits in the yard at East Croydon. A. G. Ellis

On 19 June 1950 E6 class 32413 rests at home at Bricklayers Arms shed. Walter Gilburt

Three locos are at home at Bricklayers Arms on 6 April 1958. From the left they are H class 0-4-4T 31533, E6 class 32415 and E2 class 0-6-0T 32107. Maurice Dart/Transport Treasury

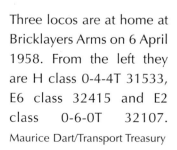

Animals in the adjacent field are oblivious to E6X class 407 as it stands at Lewes on 25 December 1918.
Locomotive Publishing Co. Ltd.

Norwood Junction's E6X class 32411 is stopped at New Cross Gate on 14 August 1955 at the head of The
Wealden Limited Railtour arranged by the RCTS. R. K. Blencowe Collection

11

Q, Q1, 700 AND 0395 CLASS 0-6-0s

These were primarily Goods locos but at times worked Passenger trains.

Nine Elms shed's Q class 30530 shunts Loco coal wagons in the shed yard in October 1964. A. R. Butcher/Top Link Photocards

At Nine Elms on 12 November 1961 are Q1 class 'Warthog' 33003 (ex C3) from Feltham and locally allocated M7 class 0-4-4T 30321. These Q1 class locos were basic utility engines devoid of all trimmings which gave easy access to fittings for maintenance. They are reputed to be the ugliest locos constructed in this country but filled an essential requirement by providing the SR with much needed heavy Goods locos. BR Standard 13T 5 plank open wagon B494087 is on the left. Maurice Dart

Feltham's Q1 class 33009 (ex C9) presents an atmospheric scene. Its safety valve blows off copious amounts of steam which is mixed with smoke from a loco behind it as it waits to go 'off shed' at Stewarts Lane on 6 April 1958. A mechanical lubricator is fitted below the smokebox above the front driving wheels. Maurice Dart

In the late 1950s Tonbridge's Q1 class 33032 (formerly C32) approaches its own station from Tonbridge North Junction.

On 8 November 1952 Nine Elms shed's 700 class 30694 approaches Clapham Junction with the 11.10am Nine Elms to Stewarts Lane Transfer Goods working. Pamlin Prints

With a tender lettered SWR 700 class 695 is at Nine Elms shed in the early 1900s before the loco was superheated. G. Smith

In the early 1950s Felthams 0395 class 30569 (previously 3163) slowly shunts wagons at Brentford. Mike Daly

12

C, C2X CLASS 0-6-0s

These mainly worked Goods services but at times of high density traffic could be seen working branch Passenger trains.

In the early 1920s C class 4 has derailed at points at Tunbridge Wells Central presenting quite a problem for the railway staff.

Two locos at home at Bricklayers Arms on 6 April 1958 are C class 31071 and N class 2-6-0 31853.
Maurice Dart

C class 31584 is at home on Stewarts Lane shed on 13 November 1960. Maurice Dart

On 11 August 1948 a fellow enthusiast poses alongside Bricklayers Arms shed's C class 1693 which is on shed at Eastbourne.

Hither Green's C class 31724 is stopped outside the east end of Dartford station on 1 September 1958. Maurice Dart/Transport Treasury

Brighton's C2X class 32442 stands outside Tunbridge Wells West shed on 3 September 1958. Its tender is a hybrid type formed by mounting a Drummond body on to a Brighton underframe. Lurking inside is local resident H class 0-4-4T 31278. Maurice Dart/Transport Treasury

Two variants of the C2X class at home on Stewarts Lane on 12 March 1939 are double-domed 2451 and single-domed 2553. R. J. Buckley/Initial Photographics

On 1 September 1958 Bricklayers Arms shed's C2X class 32553 is buffered up to local resident N class 2-6-0 31848 at Ashford shed. Maurice Dart/Transport Treasury

C2X class 32554 is at home at Bricklayers Arms on 6 April 1958. Maurice Dart/Transport Treasury

13

O, O1, EARLIER LBSC 0-6-0s AND AN LNER 0-6-0

These normally worked Goods services but were used on Passenger trains on lightly laid branch lines. The LMER locos worked cross-London Goods services

This O class A98 was withdrawn from service in October 1929 and was used to heat carriages in the sidings at Ramsgate where it was recorded in 1939. It fulfilled this duty until Summer 1953 Note the extended chimney.

Ashford's O1 class 31065 is at Rolvendon on the 3.15pm service to Headcorn on 26 October 1953. These locos retained their marvellous incongruous outside-framed tenders until withdrawal.

Three locos at Dover Marine on 1 September 1958 are residents O1 class 31065 and C class 31150 together with Stewart Lane shed's N class 2-6-0 31411. Maurice Dart/ Transport Treasury

Locally allocated O1 class 1248 shunts at the carriage shed opposite Ramsgate station in 1939.

Ashford's O1 class 31370 brings a train into Tenterden Town in 1953. A. W. Burges

In July 1946 local residents on Ashford shed are O1 class 1390 and H class 0-4-4T 1307. Locomotive & General Railway Photographs/ Real Photographs Co.

O1 class 31425 is at home on the coaling line at Dover Marine mid-evening on 1 September 1958. Maurice Dart/Transport Treasury

On 1 September 1958 O1 class 31434 is at home alongside the coal stage at Dover Marine. Maurice Dart/Transport Treasury

Outside-framed LBSC Standard Craven Goods 468 is in the yard at Brighton around 1890. The loco had been numbered 249 until October 1881 and became 515 in March 1898. Withdrawal took place in August 1898. R. Blencowe Collection

Outside-framed LBSC Standard Craven Goods 614 is at Three Bridges performing pumping duties in 1901. Previously numbered 225 this loco had been withdrawn in 1896. It worked on this duty at Three Bridges from 23 April 1897 until mid-1901. A. G. Ellis

Three locos lined up at Hither Green on 6 April 1958 are Stratford's LNER J17 class 65563, Brick-layers Arms shed's C2X class 32539 and 204hp 0-6-0 DM shunter 11221 (later D2251) which is at home. LNER 13T 6 plank vacuum fitted open wagon E45285 which was fitted with a 9ft wheelbase is on the right. Maurice Dart/ Transport Treasury

14

GWR 0-6-0 TANKS

Pannier Tanks were used on empty stock workings between Clapham Junction and Waterloo and also on cross-London Goods services. Locos from absorbed companies worked on minor railways in the area.

Old Oak Common's 8750 class 8771 brings a Goods service through Kensington Olympia in February 1961. The Westward Television launch train on the adjacent Platform line hauled by preserved 4-4-0 'CITY OF TRURO' was on display at the station from 9th to 11th of February 1961.

Still retaining its 83D (Laira) shedplate 8750 class 9770 which was allocated to Nine Elms works a short empty stock train from Waterloo through Clapham Junction on 29 February 1960. This loco was very familiar to me for many years. Ex GWR inside-framed Syphon-G W1192W is in the left background. H. C. Casserley

0-6-0ST No. 8 'HESPERUS', which the GWR sold to the Kent & East Sussex Railway in November 1912 shunts at Rolvendon on 24 September 1923. This loco which originally worked on the North Pembrokeshire & Fishguard Railway became GWR 1380 and was named 'RINGING ROCK'. It worked on the construction of the Cornwall Minerals Railway Goonbarrow branch and remained in the area for a period. Scrapping occurred in 1941. The Locomotive Club Of Great Britain/Ken Nunn Collection

KESR 0-6-0ST No.8 'HESPERUS' (ex-GWR 1380) approaches Rolvendon with a mixed train in the 1920s.

KESR 0-6-0ST No. 8, now un-named (ex-GWR 1380) stands at Headcorn in the 1930s. R. G. Jarvis/Midland Railway Trust

Ex-GWR 0-6-0ST 1386 which was sold to Bute Docks in 1911 and to the East Kent Railway later the same year is in the loco shed yard at Shepherdswell in 1936. This loco which first worked on the Whitland & Cardigan Railway became EKR No. 1 and was scrapped in 1938. To its rear in a very woebegone state is ex-LSWR 'Ilfracombe Goods' 0-6-0 0394 which was purchased by the EKR around 1916 and was partly scrapped in 1934. Jerome Ltd.

15

A1, A1X AND E1 CLASS 0-6-0 TANKS

The two classes of Terriers worked branch Passenger trains and also acted as carriage and Goods yard shunters. The E1 class mainly worked Goods services.

A1 class DS680 at Lancing Carriage Works on 19 April 1958. This loco was formerly 54 and named 'WADDON'. This loco is extant at the Canadian Historical Railway Museum.
Transport Treasury

Brighton allocated A1 class 681 (formerly named 'BEULAH') is running as a 2-4-0T at its home station around 1916. It is probably on a Kemp Town working and is coupled to LBSC 'Balloon' Brake 33. This loco was sold to the Shropshire & Montgomeryshire Railway in January 1918 and ran as their No.7 named 'HECATE'. Pamlin Prints

A1 class 'B' as Brighton Works Pilot loco in the late 1920s. Formerly numbered 82 and named 'BOXHILL' it was renumbered 380S in June 1932. Following withdrawal in 1946 it moved to the Railway Museum at Clapham and now forms part of the National Collection. F. Moore's Railway Photographs/Locomotive Publishing Co. Ltd.

A1X class DS377 as Brighton Works Pilot loco on 3 April 1958. Formerly named 'MORDEN and numbered 35 it was renumbered to 32635 in January 1959. Transport Treasury

Here is the same A1X class loco running as 32635 at Brighton shed on 21 May 1961. M. J. Jackson

A1X class 643 (formerly named Gypsyhill) is at Kemp Town with the branch train which consists of LBSC 'Balloon' Brake 1329 around 1920. This loco was sold in 1925 to the Weston, Cleveland & Portishead Railway.
Pamlin Prints

A1X class 515S converted to burn oil shunting at Lancing Carriage Works in 1946. Originally numbered 50 and named 'WHITECHAPEL' this loco worked on the Isle Of Wight as W9 where it was named 'FISHBOURNE'. On return in April 1937 it became 515S and was later altered to 32650. Named 'SUTTON' it now works on the Kent & East Sussex Railway.

A1X class 32655 at Robertsbridge on 3 July 1953 with the 8.15am train to Tenterden Town. Originally named 'STEPNEY' this loco now operates on the Bluebell Railway. R. J. Buckley

A1X class DS681 at Lancing Carriage Works on 19 April 1958. This loco was originally numbered 59 and named 'CHEAM'. Transport Treasury

Brighton's A1X class 32662 shunts the yard at Hastings in the afternoon on 3 September 1958. It is coupled to BR Standard 20T brake van B950830. In the right fore-ground is part of SR 20T brake van S56118. Originally named 'MARTELLO' this loco has been preserved at the Bressingham Steam Museum. Mike Daly/ Transport Treasury

Preserved A1X class No.3 'BODIAM' at Rolvendon on the Kent & East Sussex Railway on 30 September 1970. This loco had been sold to the KESR in May 1901 but returned to BR at Nationalization. It is still operating on the KESR.

E1 class 128 'AVIGNON' at Littlehampton shed in the mid-1900s. Real Photographs Co. Ltd.

E1 class 2142 (originally named 'TOULON') rests at home at New Cross Gate shed on 26 September 1937.
R. J. Buckley/Initial Photographics

E1 class B690 (formerly named 'BERNE' and numbered 90) is at home on shed at New Cross Gate in the mid-
1920s. Real Photographs Co. Ltd.

16

OTHER SOUTHERN 0-6-0 TANKS

These classes were normally to be found shunting yards.

Three locos are at home at Bricklayers Arms on 6 April 1958. Foremost is E2 class 0-6-0T 32104 which is in front of E4 class 0-6-2T 32565. Bunker first is H class 0-4-4T 31533. Maurice Dart/Transport Treasury

At home at Bricklayers Arms on 6 April 1958 are E2 class 0-6-0T 32107 which is fitted with extended tanks and E6 class 0-6-2T 32415. The roof of the adjoining Locomotive Works looms above the locos. Maurice Dart

In the Summer of 1961 P class 0-6-0T 'PIONEER II' (formerly 31178) is near the Exchange sidings at Bowaters works, Sittingbourne. The tank loco, which was sold to Bowaters following withdrawal, now operates on the Bluebell Railway. To the right is Drewry 204hp class O4 0-6-0DM D2291 which was allocated to Hither Green. E. Foster

Three 0-6-0Ts are at Stewarts Lane on 6 April 1958. From the left they are locally allocated E2 class 32106 and P class 31558. On the right is the bunker and part of the cab of J50/4 class 68987 from Hornsey shed. Denis Richards

In the yard at Folkestone Junction in the 1930s is Dover's R1 class 1047. Dover shed supplied locos to the sub-shed at Folkestone which had, for many years, retained a separate allocation.

Two of Dover's R1 class with cut-down cabs are on shed at Folkestone Junction on 1 September 1958. The cabs had been cut down to permit the locos to work through the tight clearance Tyler Hill tunnel on the line from Canterbury to Whitstable. In the right background is Stewart Lane's Battle of Britain class 4-6-2 34087 '145 SQUADRON'. Maurice Dart/ Transport Treasury

Dover's R1 class 31337 shunts in the yard at Folkestone Junction on 1 September 1958. Maurice Dart/Transport Treasury

In the late 1920s the sole member of the S class, A685 (later 1685) is in the Goods yard at Bricklayers Arms which was adjacent to the large loco shed to which it was allocated. This loco was rebuilt from C class 0-6-0 685 in October 1917 specifically to shunt Bricklayers Arms yard. Real Photographs Co.

Standing by the coaling plant below one of the viaducts at home at Stewarts Lane on 15 June 1946 is T class 1602.

Ex Plymouth, Devonport & South Western Junction Railway 756 'A. S. HARRIS' is at Stewarts Lane in the yard in the early 1940s during one the brief spells when it was allocated to that shed.

0330 class 0-6-0ST 127 which was sold by the SR to the East Kent Railway in December 1925 and became EKR No.7 is at Shepherdswell in the mid-1930s. This loco was scrapped in 1941.

In the early 1920s 0330 class 0-6-0ST 409 is at home outside the old part of Nine Elms shed. Withdrawal took place in December 1924.

At home at Nine Elms shed in the late 1920s is 0330 class 0-6-0ST 410 which was withdrawn in September 1930. The dash below the number indicates that the loco has been placed on the Duplicate List.

Late in 1890 0-6-0ST 459 (Named 'SAMBO' until May 1890.) is at Brunswick Wharf, Nine Elms. This loco was built by Manning Wardle as their No. 80 in May 1863. Delivered new to John Watson & Co. of Swansea it was sold to T. Chappell in February 1868 who used it on the Stoats Nest to Warlingham Tram-

way during the construction of Caterham Asylum. On 1 March 1871 it was bought by the London, Brighton & South Coast Railway who numbered it 220 and used it as pilot loco at Brighton Works until 25 February 1874 when it was sold back to T. Chappell. It was bought by the LSWR in March 1884 who used it to shunt Poole Quay until 1890. Following an overhaul it worked at Brunswick Wharf. It was withdrawn in April 1897. Brunel University Transport Collection: Clinker Views

17

4-4-2s AND 4-4-2 TANKS

The Atlantics worked express trains between London and Brighton and also Newhaven Boat Trains. The 4-4-2Ts were employed on main line and branch Passenger services.

Shortly after it was constructed in December 1905 H1 class 37 (became 2037) is posed for a 'Record Photo' at Brighton Works. As is usual with photos of this type the background has been 'Blanked Out'. The loco was allocated to Brighton and was named 'SELSEY BILL' in March 1926. London, Brighton & South Coast Railway Co.

In July 1947 H1 class 2039 'HARTLAND POINT' (It was named 'LA FRANCE' for a short period) entered Brighton Works to be modified and fitted with sleeve valve gear as a test bed for the forthcoming unconventional Leader class locos emerging from the Works in November of that year. It is in steam at Brighton shed around 1948/49.

On 24 July 1948 modified H1 class 2039 'HARTLAND POINT' stands outside Brighton Works. Brunel University
Transport Collection: Clinker Views

In the early 1920s Brighton's H2 class B421 (later 2421) heads the Southern Belle Pullman train near Merstham.
This loco was named 'SOUTH FORELAND' in February 1926. Pamlin Prints

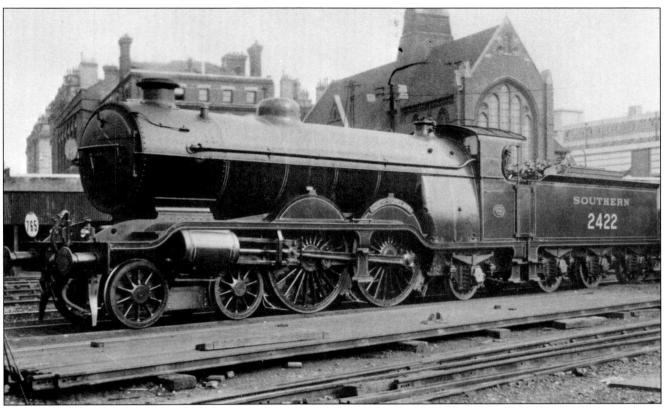

In the late 1930s H2 class 2422 'NORTH FORELAND' from New Cross Gate shed waits to depart from Brighton. This was the only member of the class to be fitted with modified framing behind the buffer beam.

Brighton's H2 class 32424 'BEACHY HEAD' is on shed at Norwood Junction in the early 1950s. J. Scrace

Around 1946 Brighton's H2 class 2425 'TREVOSE HEAD' passes through East Croydon with a Down Newhaven boat train. Pamlin Prints

0415 class 171 (became 0171 in August 1904) is at home at Nine Elms shed on 14 April 1900. This loco was withdrawn in October 1921. Are the smartly dressed gentlemen Railway Officials or visiting enthusiasts? I suspect the former from their pose. R. A. Emmerson/Pamlin Prints

0415 class 0488 running as East Kent Railway No. 5 at Sheperdswell in the late 1930s. This loco was hired for use at the Woolmer Instructional Railway at Longmoor during the First World War and in September 1917 it was sold to the Ministry Of Munitions who numbered it 27 and used it at Ridham Salvage Depot near Sittingbourne. In April

1919 it was bought by the East Kent Railway. In the mid-1940s the SR, suffering a shortage of suitable locos to work on the branch line from Axminster to Lyme Regis, re-purchased the loco in March 1946. It was numbered 3488 (later 30583) and following withdrawal it was purchased by the Bluebell Railway on 9 July 1961.

In the mid-1940s I1X class 2002 from Tunbridge Wells West shed rests at Brighton station.

Three Bridges shed's I1X class 2599 shunts in the yard at Tunbridge Wells West on 9 August 1947. Withdrawal took place in September 1948. MR 10T 5 plank open wagon LMS 62296 is in the right.

Four locos are lined up stored out of use at Guildford shed in July 1949. From the left they are L11 class 4-4-0 436 which was unallocated, I2 class 4-4-2T 2013 running as WD 72400, L12 class 4-4-0 30416 which is at home and I2 class 4-4-2T 2019 running as WD 72401. Following withdrawal in January 1939 and November 1937 and use as air raid shelters at Bournemouth Central shed 2013 and 2019 were sold to the WD on 4 March 1942. They became 2400 and 2401 and were used to work Passenger trains between Bordon and Longmoor. 2400 was named 'EARL ROBERTS' and 2401 was due to be named 'KINGSLEY' but this did not take place. Both were withdrawn in October 1946. Kenneth Brown

Battersea Park shed's I2 class 15 (became 2015) passes Belmont working the LBSC Royal Train to Epsom Downs for Epsom Races around 1912. This loco was withdrawn during January 1936. Pamlin Prints

18

SCHOOLS CLASS 4-4-0s

These fine locos worked heavy Passenger trains throughout the area.

On 1 September 1958 Eastleigh shed's 30905 'TONBRIDGE' is ex-Works on shed at Ashford awaiting a Running-in turn. It is fitted with a Self Trimming tender. In the right distance at home is L1 class 4-4-0 31758. Maurice Dart/Transport Treasury

Three locos are at home on shed at Bricklayers Arms on 6 April 1958. On the left is Fairburn 4MT 2-6-4T 42081. The main subject is Schools class 30931 'KING'S WIMBLEDON' which is fitted with a large diameter chimney. Visible inside the shed is the front of Schools class 30928 'STOWE'. Denis Richards/Transport Treasury

On shed at Ashford on 1 September 1958 is 30932 'BLUNDELLS' from Bricklayers Arms. At home on the right in the distance is N class 2-6-0 31405.
Maurice Dart/Transport Treasury

Shortly following transfer 30935 'SEVENOAKS' is at home on Nine Elms shed on 12 November 1961. Maurice Dart

Early in 1951 painted in early lined black livery Bricklayers Arms shed's 30936 'CRANLEIGH' is on shed at Stewarts Lane. The tender is devoid of any identity such as crest or name of company. In the left background is ex PDSWJR 0-6-0T 30756 'A. S. HARRIS'.

On 11 June 1939 Bricklayers Arms shed's 937 'Epsom' was fitted with an extended smokebox, a Lemaitre blastpipe and a large diameter stovepipe chimney. In this condition it is on shed at Nine Elms on 11 June 1939.
The Locomotive Club Of Great Britain/Ken Nunn Collection

19

T9, L12, S11, C8, T3 AND X6 CLASS 4-4-0s AND E10 CLASS 4-2-2-0s

In their prime these were express Passenger locos but with the building of more powerful modern classes they were relegated to working lighter stopping services.

T9 class E118 and E730 head an Up train past Esher in July 1931. Photomatic

In the late 1930s Salisbury's T9 class 122 rests at Littlehampton shed. Real Photographs Co. Ltd.

In the early 1930s T9 class 281 from Stewarts Lane shed heads a Down excursion train to Ramsgate near Teynham. Real Photographs Co. Ltd.

In the mid-1900s un-rebuilt T9 class 311 is on shed at Nine Elms as the crew pose for the photographer. Pamlin Prints

Un-rebuilt T9 class 714 is on shed at Nine Elms in the mid-1900s.

A line of locos at Brighton shed in the mid-1950s are, from the right, Fratton's T9 class 30729, Guildford's M7 class 0-4-4T 30246 and H2 class Atlantic 32424 'BEACHY HEAD'. A BR standard sludge wagon is on the right.
Rail Archive Stephenson (Photomatic)

On 24 April 1902 T9 class 773 rests at Nine Elms shed. In December 1924 this loco was renumbered to 733.
A. G. Ellis

Around 1946 Bournemouth's L12 415 moves around the yard at Nine Elms shed.

On 29 July 1953 S11 class 30400 is at home at Guildford shed alongside Feltham's H16 class 4-6-2T 30519.

Feltham's C8 class 298 is at home on 30 March 1935. This loco was withdrawn in February 1938. J. G. Sturt Collection

T3 class 574 is at home on shed at Guildford in 1932. Withdrawal took place in July 1933. The shed and yard were very conveniently situated parallel with one of the station platforms. Locomotive & General Railway Photographs/Real Photographs Co./David & Charles.

In the early 1930s X6 class 660 is at home at Feltham shed. This loco was withdrawn during October 1936.

E10 class 'Double-Single' 4-2-2-2 370 is at home at Nine Elms shed in the mid 1900s. Following withdrawal in September 1926 the boiler was sent to Lancing Carriage Works for stationary duty in August 1930. In the left background, also at home, is 460 class 4-4-0 470 which was withdrawn during February 1926.

In the mid-1900s 'Double-Single' E10 class 4-2-2-2 373 is at home on shed at Nine Elms. This loco was withdrawn during April 1927. Photomatic

20

B1, B2, B4, D, D1, E, E1, F, F1, G, L AND L1 CLASS 4-4-0S

These were mainly used on Passenger trains starting with express workings in their early days and latterly on light stopping workings.

To mark the centenary of the opening of Ashford Works an exhibition was held there in 1947. One of the exhibits was B1 class 1441 which had been withdrawn from Dover shed in August of that year. This loco was loaned to the LMS between November 1941 and December 1944 when together with 1446 it was allocated to Shobnall shed, Burton-on-Trent and worked stopping trains to Birmingham New Street.

Stewart Lane shed's B1 class 1450 is on shed at Ashford on 25 June 1939. Withdrawal took place in June 1948. J. G. Sturt Collection

B2 class 206 'SMEATON' at home at Battersea Park shed in the early 1900s. Rebuilt to a B2X class in January 1909 this loco was withdrawn in July 1933. On 2 October 1898 it worked the first 60 minute Brighton Pullman train. A. C. Hook/Pamlin Prints.

Eastbourne shed's B4 class 2057 (originally named 'BULLER') is on shed at New Cross Gate on 14 June 1936. Withdrawal took place two months later. Brunel University Transport Collection: Locomotive Views

Fratton's B4 class B69 (later 2069 and once named 'BAGSHOT') is on shed at New Cross Gate in the early 1930s. Withdrawal occurred in August 1934. Real Photographs Co. Ltd.

Ashford shed's D class 31477 backs on to a train formed of carmine-and-cream liveried stock at its home station on 11 July 1950.

D class 31501 is in use as a stationary boiler at Ramsgate shed on 1 September 1958. Withdrawn in March 1953 from Gillingham shed it took up duty at Ramsgate shed in the summer of that year. It was scrapped in a siding at Margate in January 1961. To its right at home is Schools class 4-4-0 30914 'EASTBOURNE'. Maurice Dart

D class 727 (later 1727), which was allocated to Cannon Street, heads a long westbound boat train at Folkestone Warren in the early 1900s. This venerable loco was rebuilt to a D1 class in October 1922, being withdrawn on 18 March 1961. The Knight Series.

Three locos are at Bricklayers Arms shed on 6 April 1958. At home is the main subject which is D1 class 4-4-0 31247 and on the left E6 class 0-6-2T 32410. Looking out of the shed is Gillingham's L1 class 4-4-0 31785.
Maurice Dart/Transport Treasury

D1 class 31509 is at home at Faversham shed on 6 September 1958. Maurice Dart/Transport Treasury

Redhill shed had two visitors in the morning on 2 September 1958. Against the buffers with its driving wheels removed is Ashford's D1 class 31727. In the distance beyond the Ash Shelter is Guildford shed's Q1 class 0-6-0 33025. Maurice Dart/Transport Treasury

Around 1946 Redhill's E class 1157 is on shed at Bognor Regis.

In the early 1920s E class 273 (later 1273) is on shed at Stewarts Lane. Real Photographs Co.

E class 1275 is on shed at Ramsgate in the mid-1920s.

In June 1923 E1 class 165 (became 1165) is in the yard at Stewarts Lane shed. Real Photographs Co.

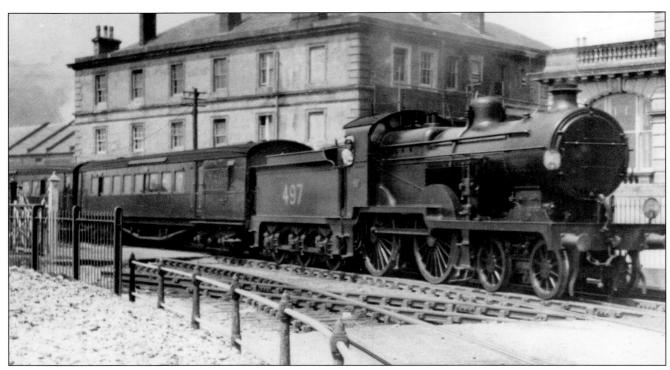

On 16 June 1924 SECR liveried E1 class 497 (became 1497) brings the first portion of the 11am boat train (the predecessor of the Golden Arrow) into Dover Marine. Pamlin Prints

On 11 June 1929 F class A421 stands on one of the Through lines at Ashford station. This loco which retains its original Stirling cab was withdrawn in March 1930. Pamlin Prints

F1 class 1060 is at Ashford with a Down service in the mid-1920s. Later rebuilt to an F1 class this loco was withdrawn in April 1946.

Reading's F1 class 1060 is on the scrap road at Ashford Works in 1946, having been withdrawn in April of that year.

F1 class 1249 is on shed at Ashford in the mid-1920s. The loco was withdrawn in June 1924. J.G. Sturt Collection/Oakfield Films

G class A680 waits at Maidstone West on a local train on 23 April 1927. These locos, which were a Great North of Scotland Railway type, were bought from that railway's builders. Withdrawal took place in September of that year.

Tonbridge's L class 31760 rests in the yard at Ashford shed on 1 September 1958. Maurice Dart/Transport Treasury

Stewart Lane's malachite-green liveried L class 1764 is on shed at Ashford in 1946.

At home at Faversham on 6 September 1958 is L class 31767. D1 class 31494 and N1 class 2-6-0 31903 stand behind.
Maurice Dart/Transport Treasury

Two locos at home at Ashford shed moving around the yard on 1 September 1958 are L1 class 31782 and N class 2-6-0 31400. Maurice Dart

21

M7, O2 AND T1 CLASS 0-4-4 TANKS

These worked Suburban and branch Passenger trains.

Around 1910 M7 class 21 waits on a local train at Kensington Addison Road.

On 9 April 1928 M7 class 29 fitted with Motor Train equipment waits to depart on a local train from Ascot.

M7 class 106 is on shed at Nine Elms around 1920. In March 1961 this loco changed identities from 30106 and emerged from Eastleigh Works as 30667.

In the early 1910s M7 class 107 is at home at Nine Elms shed.

At home on shed at Nine Elms in the early 1910s is M7 class 109. G. Smith

Three Bridges shed's Motor fitted M7 class 30110 sits alongside the coal stage at Horsham shed on 2 September 1958. I had just travelled to Horsham behind this loco on the 5.04pm from Guildford.
Maurice Dart/Transport Treasury

Around 1920 Nine Elms shed's M7 class E126 moves stock through Clapham Junction. In July 1921 this loco was rebuilt with an extended smokebox, a stovepipe chimney and other modifications including superheating but was withdrawn in May 1937.

On 23 April 1939 Nine Elms shed's M7 class 672 is stopped at Brookwood with a special train to Bisley Camp. M7 class 242, also from Nine Elms shed was on the rear of the train. The fare was 7 shillings and 6 pence return from Waterloo to Brookwood from where a one-coach shuttle train operated to and from Bisley Camp. M7 672 was withdrawn in May 1948 after falling down the Waterloo & City Railway lift shaft in the yard on the west side of Waterloo Station. R. K. Blencowe Collection

Feltham's O2 class 30179 rests at home in the evening on 31 August 1958. To the right also at home is S15 class 4-6-0 30840. Maurice Dart/Transport Treasury

Nine Elms shed's T1 class 76 arrives at Feltham on a train to Staines in 1928.

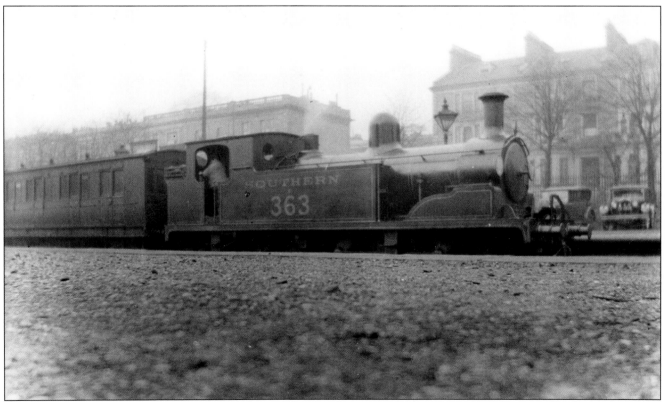

T1 class 363 from Nine Elms shed is stopped on a local train at Kensington Addison Road in November 1928. Withdrawal occurred in June 1948. Locofotos/J. A. G. H. Coltas

22

H, R, D3 AND Q CLASS 0-4-4 TANKS

These usually worked local and branch Passenger trains.

Four locos are on shed at Ashford on 1 September 1958. From the left they are locally based H class 0-4-4Ts 31522 (push-pull fitted) and 31005 (Not push-pull fitted), Tonbridge's C class 0-6-0 31272 and N class 2-6-0 31404 which is at home. Maurice Dart

Two locos at home on shed at Ashford on 1 September 1958 are N class 2-6-0 31848 and push-pull fitted H class 0-4-4T 31263. Maurice Dart/Transport Treasury

At home at Ashford shed on 1 September 1958 are, from the left, N class 2-6-0 31404, push-pull fitted H class 0-4-4T 31276 and Fairburn 4MT 2-6-4T 42098. Maurice Dart

Tonbridge shed's H class 31518 is at Westerham on the branch Motor train on 3 September 1961. Pamlin Prints

D3 class E375 (once named 'GLYNDE' and later numbered 2375) rests at New Cross Gate shed in the late 1920s. The fireman is sorting coal in the bunker of the loco which was withdrawn in May 1935. On the right can be seen the end door of a Stephenson Clarke Private Owner Mineral wagon 5189. Note the number 17 on the arm of the signal denoting which road the train is taking. *Real Photographs Co. Ltd/Ian Allan Ltd*

D3 class 2393 from Tunbridge Wells West shed is on shed at Brighton in the late 1930s.

Around 1920 Q class 23 rests at Ashford shed. Withdrawal took place during December 1928.

Gillingham's motor-fitted R class 1658 moves it train out of Chatham around 1946.

23

2-4-0s AND 2-4-0 TANKS

These normally worked Passenger trains.

Vesuvius class 280 (named 'PERSIA' for a time) at home at Nine Elms shed in 'as built' condition some time between February 1873 and April 1886 when it was rebuilt. This little loco was withdrawn in May 1896.

LC&D Railway Europa class 53 (was named 'EUROPA' and became SECR 512) at Stewarts Lane shed following rebuilding in May 1892. Withdrawal took place in April 1909. During its life this loco ran 1,048,134 miles. Real Photographs Co.

LCDR Europa class 56 'AMERICA' (became SECR 515) near Folkestone before rebuilding in November 1892. This loco was withdrawn in December 1907. Locomotive & General Railway Photographs/David & Charles/Real Photographs Co

Craven 'West End Well' 2-4-0T 12 stands alongside the soon-to-be-replaced Lovers Walk signal box, Brighton in 1882. Later this loco was numbered 131 and after rebuilding became 378. It was withdrawn during January 1889. Lens Of Sutton/Pamlin Prints

A Standard 2-4-0WT that appears to be 262 (barely readable on the burnished cabside) is at Nine Elms shed in the 1880s. This loco worked until February 1898. A. R. Kingdom

24

0-4-2s AND 0-4-2 TANKS

These normally were used on Passenger services.

A12 Jubilee class 617 is on shed at Nine Elms on 30 May 1937. This Adam's loco, fitted with a Drummond boiler, was withdrawn in October 1938. In the left background is M7 0-4-4T 32. J. G. Sturt Collection

Around 1910 Gladstone class 183 'GEORGE. A. WALLIS' is stopped on a train at Barcombe. This loco worked until February 1923. Pamlin Prints

Horsham's D1 class 2252 is stopped on a train at Southwater on the Steyning line on 1 April 1950. Pamlin Prints

D1 class 2359 (named 'EGMONT' for a while) in use as a mobile boiler washer at Dover Marine shed in the summer of 1950. Final withdrawal occurred in July 1951. Kenneth Brown

25

0-4-0 TANKS

These could be found employed as shunters in Goods yards where tight curves existed and were also used a shed Pilots.

B4 class 30084 rests at home in the yard at Dover Marine shed in the evening on 1 September 1958. This loco was very familiar to me as it was shedded at Plymouth Friary until its surprise transfer to Dover in December 1951. The loco is coupled to LMS 13T 5 plank open wagon M270233. Maurice Dart/ Transport Treasury

Guildford's B4 class 30086 (named 'HAVRE' for many years) rests inside one of the bays at its home shed on 2 September 1958. It was based at Guildford for shed pilot duties. Maurice Dart/Transport Treasury

When the requirement for the B4s to work at Southampton Docks ceased 89 'TROUVILLE' was transferred to Stewarts Lane shed. However before arriving at Stewarts Lane it is on shed at Brighton on 10 May 1947. Note the chalked on name 'THE BLACK KNIGHT' on the Smokebox door and the steam heating equipment. A. G. Ellis

In mid-1939 B4 class 91 is at home in the yard at Stewarts Lane shed. Shortly after this date this loco was transferred to Plymouth Friary and was another member of the class which I saw many times. B. Roberts/J. A. Peden

On 1 July 1905 B4 class 92 is at home outside the Roundhouse at Nine Elms shed. Side chains are fitted inside the buffers. After this loco was withdrawn it was sold to the Ministry of Fuel & Power and worked at Darton Opencast Disposal Point, near Barnsley and was scrapped there in June 1961. The Locomotive Club of Great Britain/Ken Nunn Collection

B4 class 98 'CHERBOURG' which is fitted with steam heating equipment is at home on shed at Nine Elms in August 1948. Withdrawn in February 1949 this loco was sold and worked at Stewarts & Lloyds. Bilston, Staffordshire where it was scrapped in August 1958. A. G. Ellis

Lettered SWR B4 class 103 is at home on shed at Nine Elms on 27 April 1901. This loco was a long term resident of Plymouth Friary shed so I saw it regularly. Following withdrawal in May 1949 this loco was sold to the Ministry Of Fuel & Power and worked at Backworth Opencast Disposal Point, Northumberland until it was scrapped there in August 1953.

The Locomotive Club of Great Britain/Ken Nunn Collection

On 1 September 1952 the allocated shed pilot at Guildford was 0-4-0ST 30458 'IRONSIDE' In the left background, also at home, is T9 class 4-4-0 30313. LMS 13T 5 plank open wagon M34236 is on the right.

Crane tank 1302 was taken into service stock in June 1929 and was renumbered 234S. As such it worked at Lancing Carriage Works but at the end of November 1938 it was repaired and transferred to Stewarts Lane to work at the adjacent Co-operative Wholesale Society's Milk depot. Still numbered 234S it is working at the depot in 1938. Shortly it regained its original number of 1302.

Stewarts Lane's crane tank 1302 shunts at the milk depot in the mid-1940s. It was scrapped in July 1949.
Colling Turner Photos Ltd

26

DEPARTMENTAL LOCO, SHED SCENE AND STEAM RAILCARS

This 4wDM loco at Lancing Carriage Works in the late 1950s is DS 499 although it appears to be numberless. It carries the legend 'SOUTHERN RLY' on a plate affixed to the top front of its radiator bonnet. This machine was built at Lancing Carriage works in 1935 possibly utilising the frame from a 15-ton Goods brake van. The rear radiator was a dummy. The loco was used to move carriages between different roads in the repair sheds at the east end of the Works. D. J. W. Brough

Four locos are at home around the turntable at Guildford shed on 1 September 1952. From the left they are M7 class 0-4-4T 30324, 0-4-0ST 30458 'IRONSIDE', T9 class 4-4-0 30310 and U class 2-6-0 31627.

Drummond's 4-2-4T LSWR Steam Inspection Saloon 733 affectionately called 'THE BUG' is stopped at the Down platform at Hounslow in the early 1900s. This vehicle was built at Nine Elms in 1899 and in 1916 it was put to store at Eastleigh. It was not scrapped until 24 August 1940.

Around 1905 4-2-4T 733 'THE BUG' is stopped at Clapham Junction with a member of staff standing on the buffer beam while (possibly) a Mr Drummond wearing his bowler hat stands smiling on the platform.

LSWR Steam Railmotor No.1 moves off from Hounslow & Whitton for Gunnersby around 1910. It was withdrawn in November 1916 and the loco section was scrapped. The carriage section was converted for push-pull use and fitted with electric lighting.

Sentinel-Cammell Steam Railbus No. 6 rests at The Dyke at the top end of the 1 in 40 graded curving branch line from Hove in 1933. After lingering at Ashford Works for several years it was officially withdrawn in January 1942. This branch line closed on 1 January 1939.

A panorama of the old station at Ramsgate Harbour in the early 1920s. The signal box is prominent and two 4-4-0s are present. Renamed from Ramsgate and St Lawrence-On-Sea on 1 July 1889 this station closed completely on 2 July 1926.

27

DIESEL AND ELECTRIC LOCOMOTIVES

This is a selection of Diesel shunting and main line Diesel and Electric locomotives that worked in the area covered in this book.

Ex SR 350hp 0-6-0 Diesel Electric shunter 15201 is at home at Norwood Junction shed in March 1958. Originally numbered S 1 it simply carried 1 for many years. This loco was loaned to the War Department from March 1941 until may 1945. In the right background, also at home is C2X class 0-6-0 32545. Real Photographs Co. Ltd.

Originally numbered S 2 followed by 2, 350hp 0-6-0 Diesel Electric shunter 15202 is at home on shed at Hither Green in April 1958. Loaned to the War Department from March 1941 until February 1945 this loco worked on the Western Region from April 1951 until October 1953. P. H. Groom

Originally numbered S 3 followed by 3, the third of the SR's 350hp 0-6-0 Diesel Electric shunters, 15203 rests in a siding in the large Norwood Junction yard adjacent to the depot where it was allocated. It is coupled to LNWR 10T 4-plank open wagon M25929. As with the other pair this loco was loaned to the War Department from April 1941 until April 1947 and later worked on the Western Region from May 1951 until July 1953. Mike Daly

500hp 0-6-0 Diesel Mechanical shunter 11001 rests in store at Ashford Works in 1959. It is coupled to BR Standard 42T Bogie Plate wagon B947007. Rex Conway Collection

Stewart Lane depot's 1550hp Bo-Bo 'Slim Jim' Diesel Electrics 33205 (formerly D6590) and 33203 (formerly D6588) load trains on to an SNCF Ferry at Dover Marine on 23 May 1988. 33205 was renumbered to 33302 on 18 July 1988 but reverted back to 33205 on 16 October that year.

Bo-Bo 240hp Electric DS 74 was built by the LSWR in 1899 for use on the Waterloo & City Railway. In 1915 the loco was transferred to work at Durnsford Road Power Station near Wimbledon. Renumbered 74S it is in one of the sidings alongside the power station in the mid-1950s. E. Foster.

As photos of this loco are quite rare I make no excuse for including three shots of it. In the 1950s 74S shunts Ccoal wagons at Durnsford Road Power Station. Two wagons in the left background are Maltby Colliery 13T 8-plank mineral wagon 1994 and Glasshoughton Coking Plant 13T 7-plank mineral wagon 675. Behind the loco is brand new Ministry

of Transport 16T steel mineral wagon MOT34304 which has pressed-steel side doors and is painted in bauxite livery. E. Foster

On 21 May 1955 74S appears to be at the west end of the sidings at Durnsford Road Power Station. A. G. Ellis

Seemingly devoid of a bodyside number Brighton's 1470hp Co-Co Electric CC1 (became 20001) stands by the yard outside its home station on 26 March 1942.
Southern Railway

Durnsford Road's 1470hp Co-Co Electric CC1 heads a mixed Goods train on the Quarry Line between Quarry tunnel and Redhill tunnel in the late 1940s.
Southern Railway

Hauling what appears to be a Pullman train, Durnsford Road allocated 1470hp Co-Co Electric 20001 passes through Tattenham Corner in the early 1950s. Note the bi-directional signal arms some of which carry road numbers, fitted to the gantries.

Stewarts Lane's 1470hp Co-Co Electric 20002 1470hp awaits departure on an Up express from Brighton in the mid-1950s. E. Foster

1470hp Co-Co Electric 20002 (ex CC2) rests at home at Stewarts Lane shed on 13 November 1960. Maurice Dart

Stewart Lane's 1470hp Co-Co Electric 20003 heads a Goods train through Three Bridges in mid 1959. Rex Conway Collection

2300hp Bo-Bo Electric E5013 (later 71013) from Stewarts Lane depot stands at Three Bridges in April 1963.
P. H. Groom

Chart Leacon depot's 2300hp Bo-Bo Electric E5014 (became 71014) heads a mixed Goods though Petts Wood in July 1969. P. H. Groom

Stewart Lane's 1420/600hp Bo-Bo Electro-Diesel E6005 (became 73005) rests at its home depot in May 1963. P. H. Groom

28

MISCELLANEOUS LOCOMOTIVES AND RAILWAYS

This section includes a variety of scenes from some of the many passenger and freight carrying minor railways which operated in the area covered by this book.

On 10 September 1921 0-4-0ST 'HUSTLER' is at the works of the Associated Portland Cement Co. at Swanscombe. Unfortunately it has proved impossible to read the details on the builder's plate on the side of the locomotive. The Locomotive Club Of Great Britain/Ken Nunn Collection

Standard gauge 0-4-0ST 'JUBILEE' (WB 2542/1936) is at Bowaters works at Sittingbourne in September 1961 during a visit by a group of railway enthusiasts. On the right is the rear of BR 204hp 0-6-0 DM D2291 from Hither Green shed. E. Foster

Bowaters operated an internal 2ft 6in gauge railway which ran north from Sittingbourne to Ridham Dock, part of which has been preserved and operates to Kemsley Down. In September 1961 2-4-0 Fireless 'UNIQUE' (WB 2216/1923) rests on a siding at Sittingbourne. This loco is still extant on the Sittingbourne & Kemsley Light Railway but is currently out of use. E. Foster

In September 1961 Bowater's 0-6-2T 'SUPERB' (WB 2624/1940) is at Kemsley Down. This loco remains on the S&KR. E. Foster

In September 1961 with the photographer's wife who is carrying a camera, two of Bowater's 0-6-2Ts, the nearest of which is 'ALPHA' (WB 2472/1932) are at Kemsley Down This loco is out of use on the S&KR. E. Foster

In September 1961 Bowater's 0-6-2T 'TRIUMPH' (WB 2511/1934) hauls a loaded train from Sittingbourne through Kemsley Down. This loco remains on the S&KR. E. Foster

Bowater's 0-6-2T 'CONQUEROR' (WB 2192/1922) moves empty wagons alongside transhipment sheds at the riverside wharf at Ridham Dock. This loco has been preserved and forms part of the Phyllis Rampton Narrow Gauge Railway Trust near Aberystwyth station. E. Foster.

This is a rare shot taken on 28 March 1950 of 0-4-4T 'DUNROBIN' (SS 4085/1895) in steam at Ashford shed. This loco which was owned by the Duke of Sutherland was originally housed in a shed at Golspie from where it moved to a shed at New Romney for several years before moving again to Fort Steele, Cranbrook, British Columbia. This loco has retuned home and resides at Beamish Museum. The Locomotive Club Of Great Britain/Ken Nunn Collection

This is an unusual shot of 0-4-0 Petrol Electric 'AMOS' during demolition work in inclement weather on an unknown date at Elsted, on the line from Petersfield to Midhurst, which closed on 7 September 1955. This loco was built at Clay Cross works for the 2ft gauge Ashover Railway which closed on 31 March 1950. It appears to have been adapted to operate on Standard gauge track. A. F. E. Field

In September 1923 Ford Railmotor set No.1 is running through hop fields approaching Rolvendon on the Kent & East Sussex Railway. This set was withdrawn around July 1932 and the two body sections were sold separately on 30 July 1932 and on 26 January 1935 for the princely sum of 10 Shillings each.

Kent & East Sussex Railway Shefflex twin car Railmotor No.3 stands at Headcorn around 1930. This set became No.2 when the two Ford Railmotor sets were sold. It was last used 8 March 1938, the body being sold on 8 August 1939.

Fitted with an instanter coupling, Romney Hythe & Dymchurch Railway 0-4-0 No. 4 'THE BUG' is at Dungeness around 1930. This loco was built by Krauss at Munich in 1926 and was sold to the Belle Vue Park Railway, Belfast in 1933. It later worked on a railway in another amusement park at Belfast after which it was 'lost' for a considerable time. It was eventually discovered in Belfast buried beneath a pile of scrap and was purchased by Sir William McAlpine in 1972. It was repatriated home and has been restored to working condition on the RH&DR.

Romney Hythe & Dymchurch Railway 4-6-2 No.7 'TYPHOON' at Hythe on 1 September 1931. Originally possessing three cylinders this loco was rebuilt with two cylinders during 1936. The Locomotive Club Of Great Britain/Ken Nunn Collection

2-4-0T No.1 'CAMBER' (WB 1461/1895) at Rye on the 3ft gauge Rye & Camber Tramway on 10 April 1909. This loco was sold in 1926 and the railway closed during 1940. The Locomotive Club Of Great Britain/Ken Nunn Collection

On the Rye & Camber Tramway at Rye in 1925 2-4-0T No. 1 'CAMBER' (WB 1461/1895) stands in front of a brand new 4wPE loco which was built by the Kent Constructional Co. H. C. Casserley

In 1925 on the Rye & Camber Tramway 2-4-0T No.1 'CAMBER' (WB 1461/1895) waits for departure time at Rye.
H. C. Casserley

Rye & Camber Tramway 2-4-0T No.2 'LADY VICTORIA' (WB 1511/1895) has arrived with a train at Golf Links Station on 10 April 1909. The Locomotive Club Of Great Britain/Ken Nunn Collection

On the Rye & Camber Tramway passengers wait to board a train at Rye headed by 2-4-0T 'LADY VICTORIA' (WB 1511/1895) on 10 April 1909.
The Locomotive Club Of Great Britain/Ken Nunn Collection

On the Rye & Camber Tramway on 29 August 1931 4wPE (Kent Constructional Co. 1925) waits to depart with a train from Rye. The Locomotive Club Of Great Britain/Ken Nunn Collection

A one coach train hauled by 4wPE (Kent Constructional Co./1925) is stopped at Camber Sands on the Rye & Camber Tramway around 1930.

A lady who is possibly Mrs. Casserley poses on Golf Links Station on the Rye & Camber Tramway on 12 July 1931. H. C. Casserley.

On the Standard gauge Selsey Railway 0-4-2 'Ogee' Saddle tank No.2 (later No.3) (N 1661/1871) is in store at Selsey on 5 November 1928. This loco which was cut up shortly after this photo was taken was built as a 3ft 6in gauge 0-4-0ST for the East Cornwall Mineral Railway. This company was acquired by the Plymouth, Devonport & South Western Junction Railway who rebuilt the loco to a Standard gauge 0-4-2ST at their workshop at Callington in 1907. It was purchased by the Selsey Railway in August 1912 where it was named 'HESPERUS'. This photograph has appeared in books previously where it has sometimes wrongly been described as being 0-6-0ST 'CHICHESTER' which was written on the reverse of this print. However this caption finally identifies the loco correctly.

On the Selsey Railway 0-6-0ST No.3 (became No.2) 'RINGING ROCK' which was built by Manning Wardle in 1883 is at Chichester around 1930. The railway closed completely on 19 January 1935 and all of the equipment and stock was sold by auction in June 1936.

Loaded milk churns wait to be loaded on board the Selsey Railway's Ford twin-car Railmotor at Chalder in the late 1920s. Pamlin Prints

The Selsey Railway Shefflex twin Railmotor set, with the baggage truck between the two cars, waits to depart from Chichester station around 1930.
Steamchest Publications

On the Selsey Railway the brand new twin car Shefflex Railmotor set is running alongside Pagham Harbour between Sidlesham and Ferry Siding stations around mid-1927. The Baggage Truck is coupled to the rear of the set.

An 0-4-0D shunter owned by the Royal Army Service Corps is in the Military siding at Feltham in 1938. This loco was Works No. 22500 built by James Fowler in 1938. It became WD No. 2 followed by 70002 and then 810. It worked at Hillsea followed by Tidworth and had been removed from the stock lists by 1968. E. Foster

The 2ft gauge Volks Electric Railway at Brighton opened in 1883. It was altered to 2ft 9in gauge in 1884 and was extended. One of the cars, possibly No.5, is crossing Paston Place viaduct at Kemptown around 1910. A. L. W.

LOCATION INDEX